Staffing
Forecasting and Planning

Staffing
Forecasting and Planning

Jean M. Phillips and Stanley M. Gully

Staffing Strategically Series

Society for Human Resource Management | Alexandria, Virginia | USA
www.shrm.org | © 2009

The Society for Human Resource Management (SHRM) is the world's largest association devoted to human resource management. Representing more than 250,000 members in over 140 countries, the Society serves the needs of HR professionals and advances the interests of the HR profession. Founded in 1948, SHRM has more than 575 affiliated chapters within the United States and subsidiary offices in China and India. Visit SHRM Online at www.shrm.org.

Library of Congress Cataloging-in-Publication Data

Phillips, Jean, 1969-
Staffing forecasting and planning / Jean M. Phillips, Stanley M. Gully.
    p. cm. — (Staffing strategically series)
Includes bibliographical references and index.
ISBN 978-1-58644-158-6
    1. Personnel management. 2. Employment forecasting. 3. Manpower planning. 4. Strategic planning. I. Gully, Stanley Morris. II. Title.
HF5549.P4596 2009
658.3'01—dc22
                    2009030885

10 9 8 7 6 5 4 3 2 1   09-0476

ASSESSING EXTERNAL JOB CANDIDATES

ASSESSING INTERNAL JOB CANDIDATES

THE LEGAL CONTEXT OF STAFFING

STAFFING FORECASTING AND PLANNING

STAFFING TO SUPPORT BUSINESS STRATEGY

Contents

Introduction

Workforce planning is the foundation of strategic staffing because it identifies and addresses current and future challenges to a firm's ability to get the right talent in place at the right time.[1] Forecasting and planning can increase an organization's ability to improve its capabilities, reduce its costs, and survive any economic environment. Talent and its acquisition are investments, not costs. By enabling the firm to acquire and retain the talent it will need to execute its business strategy, staffing planning is essential to a firm's ultimate strategic execution and financial performance. Forecasting and staffing planning ensures that the right talent will be in place at the right time, and enhances the return on the firm's investment in its talent.

Despite the clear advantages of forecasting and planning, for many organizations, staffing is usually reactive and geared toward filling an open position. To maximize a firm's chances to hire the right people, and to compete successfully in a competitive global-talent arena, staffing must be strategic and proactive. Jim Robbins, president and CEO of Cox Communications, puts it this way: "We spend four months per year on the budget process, but we hardly spend any time talking about our talent, our strengths and how to leverage them, our talent needs and how to build them. Everyone is held accountable for their budget. But no one is held accountable for the strength of their talent pool. Isn't it the talent we have in each unit that drives our results? Aren't we missing something?"[2]

It is widely predicted that organizations will face a challenging labor situation for many jobs in the coming years due to projected Baby Boomer retirements and lower birth and immigration rates. As a result, some organizations may be unable to staff current operations or to expand. The competition for good employees is particularly fierce for smaller companies that, despite providing the majority of new jobs in the United States,[3] may have a more difficult time hiring in general. Forecasting and planning lets firms better manage both talent shortages and surpluses. By understanding business cycles, business needs, current talent in the firm, and pipelines of future talent, human resources can proactively reduce the impact of talent competition, instead of just reacting when talent surpluses or shortages occur.

The availability of the talent needed to execute a desired business strategy will influence whether that strategy is ultimately successful.[4] A company thinking about diversifying and adding new products or services should first consider staffing loads, the current capabilities of its workforce, and the ability of current employees to learn any necessary new skills.[5] If a company does not currently have, or if it cannot obtain the talent it needs to execute its diversification strategy, it is unlikely to succeed. Similarly, a manufacturing organization that can't hire the workers it needs to execute its labor-intensive strategy may be forced to change its business strategy, adopt slower growth goals, or manufacture a different product requiring more readily available skills. A shortage of skilled labor may even require large investments of capital to automate the manufacturing processes to reduce the organization's need for skilled labor. In labor-intensive organizations such as health care, care may be denied, hospital beds may be closed, and limited opportunities for outpatient care could occur without the needed professional and technical staff. Internal and external forecasting and planning enhance an organization's ability to match its staffing practices to its strategic needs. Table 1 summarizes some common goals addressed by staffing forecasting and planning.

Table 1. Common Goals of Staffing Forecasting and Planning

1. Maintain a flexible workforce;
2. Increase productivity;
3. Increase the company's return on its talent investment;
4. Identify coming changes in business demand;
5. Identify coming changes in the supply of talent;
6. Develop employees' capabilities and prepare them for other roles in the company;
7. Retain key talent;
8. Enhance strategic execution and improve the company's competitive advantage; and
9. Reduce overtime expenses or temporary agency costs that arise from vacant positions.

Strategic forecasting and planning involves far more than simply projecting past turnover rates to predict future staffing needs. If recognized in time, companies can head off an expected talent shortage as General Electric did in the late 1970s. GE realized that rapid external environmental changes required it to consider staffing issues earlier in its strategic planning process than was previously necessary. Recognizing that the firm's business directions implied different talent requirements in the future, GE began to invest in a campus presence that would influence the teaching of skills it felt that it would need in 10 years (rather than in the next one to three years).[6]

In this book, we discuss the importance of understanding the organization's business strategy, goals, and competitive environment to identify what talents the firm will need. Ensuring that the right people are in place at the right time requires understanding and forecasting the firm's labor demand and maintaining an awareness of relevant pipelines of labor supply and talent. Action plans can then be developed to address any gaps between labor supply and labor demand. After reading this book, you will have a good understanding of the workforce forecasting and planning process.

The Workforce Planning Process

Workforce planning is the process of predicting an organization's future employment needs, as well as the availability of current employees and external hires to meet those employment needs, develop talent capabilities, and execute the organization's business strategy. The workforce planning process typically includes five steps:

1. *Identify the business strategy and competitive advantage.* A firm's strategic vision, mission, and strategy affect current and future staffing requirements by influencing the types and numbers of employees needed. It is also important to understand the behaviors and skills your company needs from employees to execute its business strategy so that you can enhance these behaviors through talent management.

2. *Articulate the firm's talent philosophy and strategic staffing decisions.* Firms differ in their commitment to tasks such as promoting workers and retaining workers as well as in their preference for hiring people with certain skills or training them after they are hired. Because these factors influence the nature of the firm's future labor supply and the type of workers it will need, they are important to understand when forecasting and planning.

3. *Conduct a workforce analysis.* Forecast both labor demand and labor supply, and identify any gaps between the two.

4. *Develop and implement action plans.* Develop action plans to address any gaps between labor-demand and labor-supply forecasts. The action plans should be consistent with the firm's talent philosophy. If not, the talent philosophy should be refined to close the gaps. Action plans can include recruiting, retention, compensation, succession management,

and training and development. Action plans can be short-term or long-term, depending on the firm's needs and the predictability of the environment. Organizations usually develop both short-term and long-term plans, and review and update the long-term plans based on external and internal changes. Action plans to address aging workforce issues, or workforces that have a disproportionate number of similarly aged employees, may need a longer time frame, as would a strategy to redesign benefits and compensation to retain employees in tight labor markets.

5. *Monitor, evaluate, and revise the forecasts and action plans.* Evaluate the effectiveness of the workforce plan in meeting recruiting and hiring goals. As the environment changes, forecasts and action plans may need to change.

Forecasting is not an exact science; it is rare for a forecast to be exactly right. Given this uncertainty, it is usually best to construct estimates as a *range*, providing low, probable, and high estimates. Recalculate estimates as changes happen in the organization's internal and

Figure 1. Workforce Planning Process

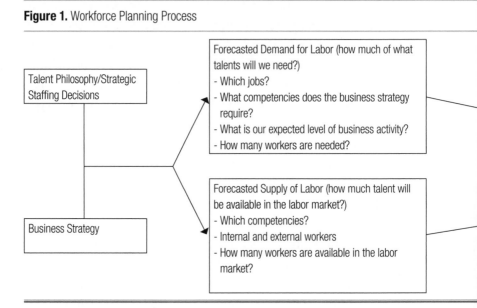

external environments and as the firm's relevant assumptions and expectations change.

Although creating forecasts and plans is easier in more stable organizations and more challenging when a company faces rapidly changing conditions, planning is most valuable for firms experiencing (or that will experience) rapid change because of the greater need to guide actions in the face of uncertainty.[7] The time frame for workforce planning should reflect the length of the business planning cycle. Business plans typically have both a long-term (e.g., three to five years) and a short-term (e.g., annual budget) component. Workforce planning typically reflects both of these time frames. Short-term workforce planning involves the necessary sourcing, recruiting, development, and separation activities to be accomplished in the coming year, although these short-term actions should also support the long-term human resource and staffing strategies.[8]

The core of the workforce planning process involves forecasting the firm's future demand for labor of different types (and the likely future supply of this labor), identifying projected labor surpluses or shortages, and developing action plans to address any forecasted talent gaps. Action

| Identify Gaps (Projected Labor Surpluses or Shortages) | Develop Action Plan(s) to Address Forecasted Talent Gaps | Monitor, Evaluate, and Revise Forecasts and Action Plans |

plans should proactively address both projected surpluses and shortages to minimize them in ways consistent with the firm's business strategy, talent philosophy, talent strategy, total compensation goals, and broader HR strategy. Figure 1 illustrated the workforce planning process.

At the very least, workforce planning should be done for those positions throughout the organization that create wealth, as well as those considered critical for the success of their unit and the firm as a whole. If innovation and intangible assets such as knowledge or creativity generate a firm's competitive advantage, then top management and knowledge workers are essential. If an organization's competitive advantage is based on service, its success depends on the quality and performance of its customer-facing employees.[9] If a vacancy in a position would create problems for the organization, then the position is a good candidate for workforce planning. The accurate identification of these key positions is extremely important, as their being vacant or poorly staffed can affect the organization's ability to perform well. Positions in which top performers significantly outperform average performers can also be important for workforce planning as these positions have the potential for above-average returns on the investment made in workforce planning. Ensuring that the most effective and productive people are placed into these positions can positively affect any company's bottom line.

We next discuss how organizations can forecast the likely future demand for their products and services, which influences their ultimate demand for labor.

Forecasting Labor Demand

The first step in the workforce planning process is to forecast the organization's demand for labor given its forecasted business activity and business needs, which depend on its business strategy. We next discuss forecasting business activity and forecasting business needs.

Forecasting Business Activity

The first requirement in projecting staffing needs is to understand the firm's likely future business activity. An organization's product demand directly affects its need for labor. If an organization is experiencing growing demand for what it does or makes, it will probably need to hire more people to meet this increased demand, unless, of course, it plans to increase the automation of its manufacturing processes. Even if the organization does plan to automate, automation may increase the demand for a different type of talent able to use and maintain the new machinery or technology even as the demand for employees with currently required skills decreases. On the other hand, if the demand for the organization's products or services is decreasing for any reason, its need for employees is likely to fall, perhaps to the point that it needs to downsize rather than hire new workers. Millions of manufacturing jobs in the United States were lost when the global demand for goods weakened after the 2001 and 2008 recessions. It is important to recognize when a decrease is short-term or long-term. For hard-to-recruit positions during short-term decrease in demand, you may need to carry people in anticipation of the rebound.

After identifying what information is needed, the next step is locating *reliable, high-quality information sources* within and outside of the organization. Accurately forecasting business activity requires identifying key factors affecting business activity, identifying quality sources of relevant forecasting information for those factors, and using these sources to compile complete, accurate, and timely data. These sources differ for different companies and different industries. For example, Cisco's visibility into expected future orders from customers and data on product availability from suppliers[10] enhanced their ability to make more accurate projections about future sales and workforce needs, and to adjust staffing needs accordingly.

The time frame for a business activity forecast is at the discretion of the organization. It may make sense for organizations in relatively stable, predictable environments to make five-year, or even 10-year, forecasts. Organizations in more dynamic, unpredictable environments may have great difficulty making reasonably accurate business forecasts for periods greater than six to 12 months out. Forecasts are best treated as dynamic estimates, and should be revisited and updated regularly as assumptions and environmental conditions change. Constructing short-, mid-, and long-range estimates is also useful because long-range forecasts are likely to be less accurate than short-range estimates due to the increased likelihood of environmental and organizational changes in the long-term.

In developing any type of forecast, the first step is to identify the types of information needed to make an accurate forecast for the type of business the company is involved in. Although many types of information may prove useful in forecasting business activity, we will next discuss five of the most common: seasonal factors, interest rates, currency exchange rates, competitive changes, and industry and economic forecasts. These are useful for evaluating general trends in business conditions and the labor market. However, they do not necessarily address trends in specific lines of business or in the specific types of future talent required.

Seasonal Forecasts. For some organizations, business demands are seasonal and predictable. For example, United Parcel Service experiences a sharp increase in shipping volume from November to January every year due to increased holiday shipping demands. Landscaping firms know that they will need more workers in the summer than in the winter. Because this increased seasonal demand occurs every year, it can be anticipated. For many organizations, business cycles are much less predictable. Occasional spikes and dips in the demand for an organization's products or services can be harder to forecast, but the better an organization can anticipate them the better it will be able to have an appropriate workforce in place.

Interest Rate Forecasts. In forecasting business activity, interest rate forecasts can project the likelihood that the organization will be able to build new plants and increase production in the near future. Higher interest rates discourage capital investment by making it more expensive for organizations to borrow money to fund their expansion plans. Because higher interest rates make goods and services more expensive for consumers who have to borrow money to afford them, product demand tends to decline when interest rates rise and it tends to rise when interest rates fall. Rising interest rates thus generally suggest declining demand for labor, and falling interest rates generally suggest an increase in labor demand. For example, when interest rates fall, the demand for homes tends to increase, increasing the demand for skilled trades workers and mortgage specialists.

Currency Exchange Rate Forecasts. For many companies, especially global ones, exchange rate forecasts may similarly be useful in making business activity forecasts. If a country's currency is strengthening against other currencies, it means that one unit of the country's currency translates into greater amounts of the foreign currency than when the country's currency was weaker. This means that the country's companies can import goods and materials more cheaply because one unit of their currency buys more foreign goods than it used to, but it also means that country's products are more expensive overseas. If a U.S. company does a lot of business internationally, a strengthening U.S. dollar may translate into decreased international demand for its products, decreasing its demand for labor. This effect was seen in New Zealand when beef jerky maker Jack Links had to cut 102 jobs, or two-thirds of its workforce, when the New Zealand dollar strengthened against the U.S. dollar and it became cheaper for its biggest U.S. customer to buy its jerky from Brazil.[11] As a country's currency weakens, prices of its exported goods fall, increasing international demand for things produced in that country and its companies' demand for labor. Exchange rates can be volatile and difficult to predict in the long-term. The more stable the exchange rate, the more accurate and useful the forecast.

Competitor Forecasts. If new competitors enter an industry or open nearby, the demand for a company's products or services may fall. Customers will have greater choice, and this increased competition will tend to decrease the demand for any one company's products or services. Alternatively, if competitors leave a company's market, then surviving companies might experience an increase in the demand for their products or services. If competition increases, the demand for a company's products or services is likely to decrease. Conversely, if competition decreases, business activity is likely to increase. In the face of increased competition from foreign carmakers, many U.S. carmakers, including General Motors and Daimler-Chrysler, experienced declining demand for their products and downsized their workforces.

Industry and Economic Forecasts. The information relevant to making a forecast is likely to differ for different companies and different industries. For some organizations, a monthly tracking of incoming orders can provide clues to the likely order volume the next month and next quarter. *The Conference Board's Index of Leading Indicators,* a commonly used barometer of economic activity over three to six months, presents a relatively broad picture of the economy and can help identify trends of economic recession or recovery. The monthly *Conference Board Consumer Confidence Index* measures consumer sentiment by asking survey respondents questions about their perceptions of their job security and willingness to spend money, which can help predict future economic activity and thus demand for a company's products and services. Additional economic indicators include gross domestic product (GDP), the business inventories/sales ratio tracked by the Department of Commerce, and the *Purchasing Managers Index* issued monthly by the Institute for Supply Management. Disappointing corporate earnings pre-announcements from a firm's own customers can also suggest a declining demand for its products.

Industries often have their own forecasts, such as the National Restaurant Association's annual industry forecast. An organization can analyze past relationships between these and other indicators to identify which ones tended to accurately predict changes in business demand and use these to predict its likely future labor demand.

Other Factors. Additional factors can also indicate changing demand for the organization's products and services, and the need for changes in the workforce. For example, many firms start hiring as the economy starts expanding so that new employees will be well trained and productive by the time the increased economic growth generates increased business activity for the firm. Some other factors that often cause companies to change the size of their workforce include:

- An increase or decrease in consumer spending;
- An increase or decrease in the unemployment rate;
- An increase or decrease in consumer disposable income;
- Increased or decreased purchases of durable goods;
- Increased or decreased housing purchases; and
- The company entering or exiting a particular line of business.

Business Needs

Business needs can include things such as:

- Achieving the staffing levels necessary for generating a given amount of revenue within a particular period of time (e.g., salesperson staffing levels necessary to generate $5 million of revenue within six months);
- Increasing staffing levels to execute a growth strategy;
- Decreasing staffing levels during a restructuring; and
- Obtaining the new talents needed to create new products or provide different services.

To better size their sales forces in each of their divisions, companies such as Whirlpool calculate the investment in human resources that would be required to reach their optimum profit level. Sizing analyses and statistical models can identify if a company is slightly overstaffed in one channel or has untapped potential in another, and predict the bottom-line impact of each salesperson added.

The most important labor-demand forecasts are often for those positions and skills that will be central to the organization's intended strategic direction. For example, assume an organization is experiencing slow growth in its bricks-and-mortar facilities but it is intending to roll out a new web-based initiative for selling its product line. Labor forecasts might indicate that overall hiring will stay relatively flat, but in light of the new strategic initiative, the company will obviously need experienced IT specialists, computer technicians, and software writers. It will also need customer service employees who are technologically competent. If it cannot hire these people, then the new web-based initiative is likely to fail.

It is a good idea to identify minimal, as well as optimal, staffing levels when analyzing labor demand. There are many ways to forecast labor demand, and we will next discuss four of the most common: ratio analysis, scatter plots, trend analysis, and judgmental forecasting.

Ratio Analysis. We can convert the estimated level of business activity into the number of employees the company will need to attain this level of productivity by using past staffing ratios or past relationships of the number of employees required to produce certain levels of output. A firm can then index the number of people it seeks to employ with the business metric. For example, a law firm might index the number of paralegals to the number of attorneys on staff at a ratio of 3:2, and employ three paralegals for every two attorneys.

Ratio analysis assumes that there is a relatively fixed ratio between the number of employees needed and certain business metrics. Using historical patterns within the firm helps to establish a reasonable range for these ratios. This process can be used for either justifying new positions or demonstrating the need for layoffs.

For example, assuming that a manufacturing facility has 100 employees and produces $20 million of product annually, then the firm's production-to-employee ratio is $200,000:1. For every additional $200,000 of product the company wants to produce, it should hire an additional worker. Because some economies of scale will result from the expansion that will reduce the number of employees needed, organizations should consider their unique situation and adjust their forecasts accordingly.

Other ratios that can be used in estimating target headcount levels include:

- Revenue per employee;
- Managers to employees;
- Inventory levels to employees;

- Store size to employees;
- Number of customers or customer orders to employees;
- Labor costs to all production costs; and
- The percent utilization of production capacity to employees.

Educated adjustments may be required to accommodate changing demographics, the impact of new technologies, and the expense of recruitment, development, and company turnover statistics when determining final numbers and costs. Involving experienced members of the management team and using past data and experience to make and adjust forecasts can enhance accuracy. The data used for any ratio must be credible and reliable, or the estimates they produce will not be used or accurate.

If an organization expects its ratio of employees to outputs to remain stable over the forecasting period, then simply applying the past ratio of employees to productivity to the forecasted business demand can be adequate. However, if the organization is experiencing a change in productivity per employee, due to technology, training, restructuring, etc., then the application of past ratios is inappropriate. Managers will often have a good idea of how estimates need to be adjusted, and their expertise should be incorporated into the process. In entirely novel situations for which past ratios do not exist, managers' judgments of the numbers and types of employees they need to get their job done may be the only way of generating a reasonable forecast. Although ratio analyses are limited to one predictor of labor demand at a time (e.g., required labor hours per unit produced), more advanced statistical techniques such as regression analysis can be used to incorporate multiple predictors (e.g., sales forecasts, store sizes, mall traffic, and seasonal trends can be used to forecast the number of employees needed in each retail store).

Forecasting labor demand in small- and medium-size organizations can be more difficult because historical trends are likely to be more variable and because there is typically less historical information from which to draw. Additionally, adding one new person in a 10-employee company means expanding the workforce in 10-percent increments, which may not map onto the growth rate of the business. Companies of all sizes may prefer to hire temporary, contingent workers or schedule overtime until they are sure they need the additional employees.

Scatter Plots. Scatter plots show graphically how two different variables (e.g., revenue and salesperson staffing levels) are related. For the purposes of forecasting labor demand, scatter plots help to determine if a factor has historically been related to staffing levels. This information is then used to determine what staffing levels should be as this factor changes.

Assume that new housing developments are being built in the area served by Ambulance Express, a private ambulance service. The company wants to forecast its future requirements for ambulance drivers and knows that the more people living in its service area, the more drivers it will need to meet the community's needs. The staffing expert first collects data from six other ambulance services in the state to learn their number of ambulance drivers and the population in their service area. Table 2 summarizes these numbers.

Table 2. Population and Required Ambulance Drivers

Population Served	Number of Ambulance Drivers
12,500	2
25,000	5
30,000	5
35,000	6
50,000	10
60,000	11

Figure 2 shows these two sets of numbers graphically in a scatter plot. The population served by the various ambulance services is on the vertical axis and the corresponding number of ambulance drivers employed by each of the companies is on the horizontal axis. Each point on the graph reflects one company. The solid line minimizes the distances between each point and the line, and reflects the predicted staffing level for each number of people served. Ambulance Express anticipates serving 43,000 people within two years. Starting on the horizontal axis, locate the point that reflects 43,000 people and draw a dotted vertical line over to the solid diagonal line. From this point on the solid diagonal line, draw a dotted horizontal line left to the vertical axis. The staffing level at which this horizontal line touches the vertical axis is the estimate of the number of ambulance drivers that will be needed for Ambulance

Express to service 43,000 people. In this example, servicing 43,000 people will require eight drivers.

Figure 2. Scatter Plot of the Relationship Between Population Served and the Number of Ambulance Drivers

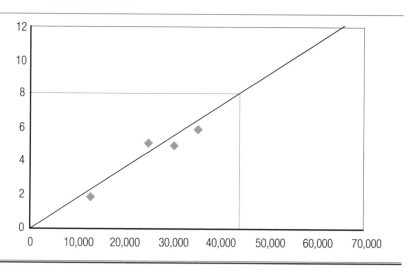

Trend Analysis. Trend analysis requires looking at past employment patterns at the employer, in the industry, or even nationally, and using them to predict future needs. For example, if a company has been growing five percent annually for the last eight years, it might assume that it will experience the same five percent annual growth for the next few years. Any employment trends that are likely to continue can be useful in forecasting labor demand. Because so many factors can also affect staffing needs, including competition, the economic environment, and changes in how the company gets its work done (e.g., automation might improve productivity), trend analysis is rarely used by itself in making labor-demand forecasts.

Valero Energy Corporation used historical trends to accurately forecast its talent demand by division and title three years in advance. By putting five years of historical employee records into a database, the company developed a series of mathematical algorithms for turnover-trend analysis by location, position type, salary, tenure, and division.[12]

Figure 3 illustrates a trend analysis using a hypothetical example of a hospital's number of internationally versus domestically educated nurses from 2001-2008. The trend lines show that the number of domestically educated nurses has been steadily declining, and the number of internationally educated nurses has been steadily increasing, over the last seven years. This suggests that the hospital might need to scale up its international recruiting efforts. International recruiting has a longer lead time, which needs to be factored into the plan.

Figure 3. Domestically and Internationally Educated Nurses (2001-2008)

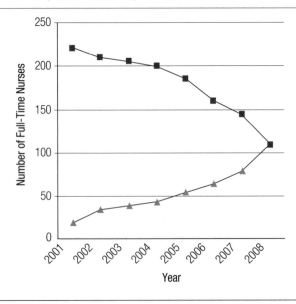

▲ Internationally Educated   ■ Domestically Educated

Judgmental Forecasting. Instead of trying to identify past relationships between staffing levels and various factors, as is the case with the previous methods discussed, judgmental forecasting relies on the experience and insights of people in the organization to predict future needs. Judgmental forecasting can be top-down, in which case organizational leaders rely on their experience and knowledge of their industry and company to make predictions about what future staffing levels will need to be. Top managers' estimates then become staffing goals for the lower levels in the organization. In some cases, particularly when companies are facing financial difficulties or restructuring, budgets may determine these headcount numbers.

Bottom-up judgmental forecasting uses the input of lower-level managers in estimating staffing requirements. Based on supervisors' understanding of the business strategy, each level provides an estimate of their staffing needs to execute the strategy. The estimates are consolidated and modified as they move up the organization's hierarchy until top management formalizes the company's estimate of its future staffing needs into staffing goals.

Because historical trends and relationships can change, it is usually best to supplement the more mechanical ratio, scatter-plot, and trend-forecasting methods with managerial judgment. Most firms use the more mechanical methods as a starting point and then use managerial input to modify the estimates.

Return-on-Investment Analysis. It is possible to estimate the return on investment from adding a new position based on the costs and outcomes resulting from that new hire. The first step is to assign dollar values to the benefits expected from a new hire for the period of time most appropriate for the position and the organization—it could be a month, a quarter, or a year. How much revenue during the period will be directly generated as a result of this position? How much money per period will this position save the organization in terms of increased efficiency, and how much value will it add in greater productivity, quality, or customer service? The sum of these figures is the value of adding this position.

The next step is to compare this amount with the cost of adding the new hire, including advertising the position, interviewing, screening, travel, relocation, training, and benefit expenses. Add the cost of hiring to the compensation for the new position during the time period used for calculating the benefits of adding the new position to identify the initial investment. Then compare this amount with the value the company will gain to determine the return on the investment of adding the new position.

For example, assume a store's new furniture salespeople generate an average of $60,000 in profit their first year. In addition, the reduced workload on the rest of the sales staff improves their efficiency and ability to provide high-quality customer service by five percent, and is worth an additional $15,000 to the company. If the cost of hiring and training a new salesperson is expected to be $7,000, and their salary is $25,000 before commissions, the return on investment of hiring an additional sales person is predicted to be 234 percent:

$$\frac{(\$60,000 + \$15,000)}{(\$7,000 + \$25,000)} =$$

$$\frac{\$75,000}{\$32,000} =$$

234% ROI

Forecasting Labor Supply

Strategic staffing requires firms to keep their fingers on the pulse of their labor markets. Knowledge of current and future trends in the labor market, broken down by skill and competency, is crucial to effective labor-supply forecasting. Information on the number and quality of employees likely to be available to an organization when it needs them should be considered while the organization is in the process of formulating its business strategy. A key driver for the success of any business strategy is the organization's ability to execute the strategy, and the nature of the organization's talent is largely responsible for this. Attempting to grow a fiber-optics division of an organization by 20 percent a year may be infeasible if sufficient numbers of fiber-optics engineers and technicians are unavailable in the labor pool at salaries it is able to pay. It is obviously best for an organization to have a reasonable estimate of the projected availability of talent for its key positions before developing a strategy that depends on this talent pool. It is particularly important for smaller firms—which often have a more difficult time hiring than do larger companies—to consider staffing issues when formulating business strategies.

Combining current staffing levels with anticipated staffing gains and losses can result in an estimate of the supply of labor for the target position at a certain point in the future. Anticipated gains and losses can be based on historical data combined with managerial estimates of future changes. The organization's internal and external labor markets will influence these estimates. The external labor market consists of people who do not currently work for a firm, and a firm's internal labor market consists of the firm's current employees. We will discuss each one next.

Forecasting the Internal Labor Market

In determining the likely supply of labor at a given time, first estimate the number of employees likely to be working for the company at the end of the forecasting period. To forecast internal talent resources for a position, subtract anticipated losses from the number of employees in the target position at the beginning of the forecasting period. These losses may be due to factors including promotions, demotions, transfers, retirements, and voluntary and involuntary terminations. In tighter labor markets when workers are harder to find, more employees than usual may leave the organization to pursue other opportunities. Fewer may leave during looser labor markets when jobs are less plentiful. Anticipated gains for the position from transfers, promotions, and demotions are then added to the internal labor-supply forecast.

Analyzing a company's demographic mix and current turnover rates can help forecast how many of an organization's current employees will likely still be in the company's workforce at the target forecasting date. Some organizations that expanded rapidly in the past may find a particularly large cohort of employees hired at roughly the same time will be retiring at about the same time, leading to an unusually large replacement need. Given their better knowledge of their subordinates, supervising managers may also be able to reasonably estimate the percentage of their current workforce likely to be with the organization at some specified date in the future. Transition analysis, managerial judgment, talent inventories, and replacement charts are some of the methods used to forecast internal talent resources. We will discuss these methods next.

Transition Analysis. In forecasting labor supply, a statistical technique called transition analysis (also called Markov analysis4) can be used to analyze internal labor markets and forecast internal labor supply. Transition analysis is a simple but often effective technique for analyzing an organization's internal labor market, which can be useful in answering recruits' questions about promotion paths and the likelihood of promotions as well as in workforce planning. Transition analysis can also forecast the number of people who currently work for the organization likely to still be employed in various positions at some point in the future. The analysis is best performed for a limited number of jobs at a time to keep it easily interpretable.

A conceptual illustration of labor-supply forecasting using transition analysis to understand the organization's internal labor market is presented in Figure 4. A transition analysis is performed by first identifying all of the positions in the company that feed employees into the target position and which employees in the target position tend to get promoted, demoted, or transferred. Ideally, all of the employees entering and leaving the target job are tracked to promote the accuracy of the transition matrix. The cells in the transition probability matrix contain the percentage of employees staying in the same job, moving to a different job in the company, or exiting the company.

Figure 4. Conceptual Illustration of Labor-Supply Forecasting Based on Internal Labor Market

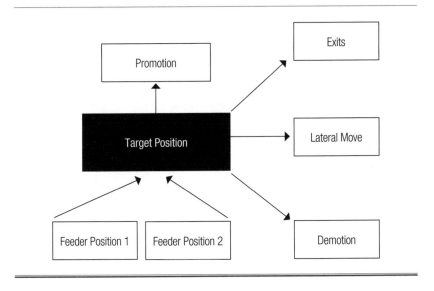

As a numerical example, assume that it is the beginning of 2010 and the company needs to do a transition analysis to forecast the likely number of employees its customer service call center will have at the beginning of 2011. Table 3 shows the transition probabilities, or the likelihood of people staying in their current position or moving, for four jobs reflecting three job levels in the organization based on the average of data from 2008 and 2009. Full-time and part-time customer service representatives are at the entry-level, supervisors are the middle job-level, and managers are at the third job-level. The last column identifies the number of employees currently working at each job at the beginning of 2010. The transition probabilities are in the third to seventh columns of the matrix and reflect the probability that an employee who begins the year employed in the job identified to the left will be employed in the job identified at the top of the column or will have exited the organization by the end of the year. The numbers on the diagonal (in bold) reflect the probability that an employee who begins 2010 in the job named to the left will still be in that job at the end of the year.

Table 3. Transition Probability Matrix

| Job Category (1) | Level (2) | Transition Probabilities (2008-09) | | | | | Current (2010) |
		FTCSR (3)	PTCSR (4)	SUP (5)	MGR (6)	Exit (7)	# of Employees (8)
Full-time Customer Service Representative (FTCSR)	1	**40%**	10%	10%	0	40%	400
Part-time Customer Service Representative (PTCSR)	1	20%	**50%**	5%	0	25%	150
Supervisor (SUP)	2	5%	0	**85%**	5%	5%	75
Manager (MGR)	3	0	0	0	**65%**	35%	20

A transition probability matrix is presented in Table 3. Reading across the first row indicates that 40 percent of the employees who begin 2010 as full-time customer service representatives are likely to still be working as customer service representatives at the beginning of 2011. Ten percent of the employees who begin the year working as full-time customer service representatives are likely to end the year working as part-time customer service representatives, and 10 percent are likely to have been promoted to supervisor. None of the employees beginning the year as a full-time customer service representative can be expected to be a manager by the end of the year. The "Exit" column reflects the percentage of employees in each job that can be expected to have left the company by the end of the year (in italics). In this case, the turnover rate among full-time customer service representatives has been 40 percent; among part-time customer service representatives it has been 25 percent; among supervisors it has been 5 percent; and among managers it has been 35 percent. When reading the table, it is helpful to remember that, for each cell, the job identified at the beginning of the row is the relevant starting position (at the beginning of the time period captured by the matrix), and the job identified at the top of the column is where employees end up at the end of the time period captured by the matrix.

The bottom row of Table 4 shows the forecasted employees in each of the four jobs for 2011. The numbers in the "Forecasted Employees Using the Transition Probability Matrix" table come from multiplying the current number of employees in each job by the transition probability in the corresponding cell in the "Transition Probabilities" matrix in Table 3. For example, multiplying the 400 current full-time customer service representative employees by 0.40 gives us an estimate of 160 of those 400 employees being in the same job at the beginning of 2011; and multiplying 400 by 0.10 gives us an estimate of 40 full-time customer service representative employees becoming part-time by 2011, and 40 being promoted to supervisor. None of the 400 employees are expected to be promoted to manager by 2007 (400 * 0). In the second row, multiplying the 150 part-time customer service representatives by 0.20 gives us an estimated 30 still in the same job in 2011, and multiplying 150 by 0.50 gives us an estimate of 75 of them becoming full-time customer service representatives by 2011. Multiplying 150 by 0.05 gives us an estimate of approximately eight of the part-time customer service representatives being promoted to supervisor by 2011, perhaps due to the completion of a degree. The numbers in bold on the diagonal reflect the number of people in each job in 2010 expected to be in the same job at the beginning of 2011. In the bottom row of the table are the column sums (in bold), which represent the number of people forecasted to be in the job identified at the top of the column at the beginning of 2011. In this case, the company can expect to enter 2011 with 194 full-time customer service representatives, 115 part-time customer service representatives, 112 supervisors, and 17 managers, based on the transition probabilities. A total of 207 employees will have left the organization.

Table 4. Forecasted Employees Using the Transition Probability Matrix

Job Category (1)	Level (2)	FTCSR (3)	PTCSR (4)	SUP (5)	MGR (6)	Exit (7)	# of Employees (8)
		Forecasted Employees for 2011					Current (2010)
Full-time Customer Service Representative (FTCSR)	1	160	40	40	0	160	400
Part-time Customer Service Representative (PTCSR)	1	30	75	8	0	37	150
Supervisor (SUP)	2	4	0	64	4	3	75
Manager (MGR)	3	0	0	0	13	7	20
Forecast for 2011		194 deficit	115 deficit	112 surplus	17 deficit	207 exits	

Comparing these estimates with the company's current staffing levels, if the company expects to maintain its current staffing levels, it is likely to have to hire from outside the organization for three of the four positions (206 full-time customer service representatives, 35 part-time customer service representatives, and three managers). For supervisors, however, the company can anticipate having 112 compared to its current number of 75. This suggests that it may be facing a surplus of 37 supervisors if past trends of internal movements and quit rates continue. This could present an opportunity to consider expansion since surplus managerial talent is expected to be available, or it could mean that alternative promotion paths have to be considered or promotion rates to supervisor positions need to be reduced to prevent the surplus.

In this example, the transition probabilities are the average movements of employees for the two years 2008 and 2009, but any meaningful period can be used in developing the transition probabilities. Some organizations face environments that are relatively stable, and will find that their transition probabilities stay relatively constant over time. In this case, accurate transition analysis results can be obtained from longer time frames. Other organizations will experience fluctuations in employee movements that make it difficult to identify relevant probabilities. In such a case, the most accurate transition analysis results are likely to come from transition probabilities derived from relatively short periods of a few months rather than a year or more. Transition analyses are most useful for larger labor forces because of the enhanced accuracy of estimation; it is less effective for very small employers. Variations of this approach can include probabilities adjusted by judgmental estimates or adjusted for growth rates in the business (e.g., recalculate deficits and surpluses to consider a 10 percent growth rate in the business).

Like any forecasting technique, transition analysis has some limitations.[13] Because transition analyses do not detect multiple moves (e.g., a person being promoted twice in the period used to generate the transition probabilities), it is best to keep the time interval used to calculate the transition probabilities to two years or less to best capture the internal labor market. If any reason can be identified for why past patterns of employee movements will change, say due to an expected pay increase or surge in employee retirements, these expectations should be factored into the transition probabilities. In some cases, past trends will not be as accurate as manager estimates, and manager input on the probability estimates may be needed before relying on them to make forecasts. This is particularly true if new strategic directions are being considered. Also, if only a few people moved into or out of a job, the transition probability estimate may be unstable and subject to error. If jobs contain a small number of employees (less than 25 or so), estimates of future availabilities are also likely to be unstable. Transition analysis also assumes that all employees in a job have an equal probability of movement. Given the number of factors organizations take into account when making movement decisions about any given employee (seniority, job performance, skill levels, etc.), the probability of movement is likely to vary across individual employees.

Despite the limitations noted above, a variety of organizations successfully use transition analysis for labor-supply forecasting. Police departments, retail companies, high-tech companies, and the military have all effectively employed transition analysis, or a variation of it, to evaluate and assess current and future hiring needs. Like budgeting, forecasting is an imperfect science, but it will generally produce meaningful and useful estimates of staffing needs. It is far better than doing nothing at all. Again, because of the uncertainties involved with forecasting, entering conservative and optimistic estimates to produce a forecasted range is likely to generate a more accurate and useful forecast than a point estimate.

Judgment. Asking managers and supervisors for their opinion on future staffing levels and employee skill levels can be very insightful. Managers are often aware of what is going on in the lives of their subordinates, and they may be able to provide reasonably accurate predictions of their future labor supply. Managers are often aware of the retirement eligibility and intentions of their staff, and can use this information to project likely talent losses due to retirement several years into the future. This type of subjective forecast may be used to supplement statistical techniques, or used instead of them if there is reason to believe that the statistical techniques will not be sufficiently accurate. Managers should be partners with the staffing planning function to the greatest extent possible in forecasting the numbers and competency levels of their employees. Although they may not realize it or be too busy to provide it, it is important that managers be willing to provide forecasting data sufficiently in advance of a hiring need to enable the staffing function to best meet the manager's hiring needs in a timely manner.

The primary limitation of all forecasting techniques is the reliance on historical patterns and activity levels: If the environment changes, past patterns may no longer hold. For example, if the unemployment rate is increasing, employees may be less likely to leave the company than they were in previous years when it was easier to find another job. On the other hand, decreasing unemployment rates may indicate that other employment opportunities exist and may lead to an increase in the number of employees quitting their jobs. This may also create a greater difficulty in attracting sufficient numbers of qualified applicants. In this case, changes in an organization's compensation policy to offer above-market wages may improve the retention of current employees and increase the organization's internal labor supply. If an organization's required competencies change, and if the current employees do not possess the skills that will be needed in the future, the organization's ability to meet its future staffing requirements decreases.

Talent Inventories and Replacement Charts. Forecasting the likely number of employees who will be available at a given time is only half of the picture. It is also important to identify which current employees might be qualified for the anticipated job openings. This requires knowledge of employees' skill sets and qualifications. Although identifying some candidates might be easy, identifying as many qualified employees as possible requires more formal planning.

Manual or computerized talent inventories summarize each employee's skills, competencies, and qualifications. They may also contain information about the employee's education and training, languages spoken, previous performance reviews, and promotability assessments. Talent inventories can be easily searched to identify which employees might be good fits for open positions, particularly if they are computerized. A talent inventory can be a powerful tool for quickly getting the right talent in the right place at the right time. The New York State Department of Taxation and Finance used an inventory system to reassign employees whose jobs were being eliminated. By allowing employees' educational and experiential backgrounds to be quickly matched with the minimum qualifications for jobs in various state agencies, the inventory allowed most displaced employees to be placed in other jobs within six weeks.[14]

Computerized talent inventory systems and HR information systems that track labor supply and talent inventories can make internal labor-supply forecasting substantially easier. Software and services allow companies to match employees' expertise and knowledge to business needs and deploy the right people just as assets would be deployed in a supply chain.[15] IBM's Workforce Management Initiative borrows many of the same concepts of supply chain management, such as capacity planning, supply and demand planning, and sourcing. IBM built a structure that outlines internal and external skills and provides a minute-to-minute view of IBM's labor supply chain using a computerized talent inventory. The software catalogs skills, creating common descriptors around what people do, what their competencies are, and what experiences and references they have—information that goes well beyond a basic job description.[16]

When it had only been deployed for a few months, IBM's labor supply chain was tested when a large client based in Washington, D.C., contacted IBM the day before Hurricane Katrina was about to hit its server hub. The client requested 14 staff with specific skills in data analysis, process improvement, logistics management, project management, and information management. A search was placed, and within 24 hours, all 14 of the individuals were in place in the requested locations to support the recovery effort. Tracking down a team without the system would have taken weeks.[17]

Replacement charts are a way to track the potential replacements for particular positions.[18] A replacement chart can be manual or automated, and shows each of the possible successors for a job and summarizes their strengths, present performance, promotion readiness, and development needs. Figure 5 gives an example of a replacement chart.

Figure 5. Replacement Chart for Future Vice President of Human Resources

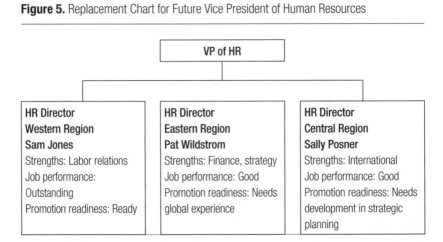

Employee Surveys. The availability of internal talent is dependent on turnover rates, which are not always constant. Conducting employee surveys and monitoring indicators of employee engagement can help to identify the potential for increased turnover in the future. That information is then used to meet with employees to work toward identifying opportunities for improvement. For organizations with a talent philosophy of retaining talent, or for organizations for which turnover is particularly harmful to business-strategy execution, staying in touch with employee and managerial attitudes can be critical to retaining the talent necessary for the firm to reach its goals.

An organization should easily be able to put together an age profile of its workforce, allowing it to forecast how much of its talent in various areas and units it is likely to lose to retirement at various points in the future. Despite the relative ease of compiling this information, 66 percent of participants in a survey by The Conference Board reported that their companies do not have an age profile of their workforce, suggesting that they lack hard data on how retirements will affect various divisions and business units. Additionally, despite their obvious usefulness for forecasting, more than 63 percent of survey respondents reported that their organizations did not have an inventory of available skills and talents, and 49 percent did no assessment of their companies' training and development needs.[19] This may be particularly problematic in coming years. According to Development Dimensions International Inc., a global human resource consulting firm, by 2011, 20 percent of large, established companies in the United States will lose 40 percent or more of their top-level talent while the replacement pool of 35- to 44-year-olds declines by 15 percent. This further increases the importance of developing proactive staffing plans.[20]

Forecasting the External Labor Market

All organizations have to hire from the external labor market at some point. In addition to needing to hire new workers to meet expanding demand, outside people need to replace current employees who retire or leave the organization for other reasons. Organizations monitor the external labor market in two ways. The first is through their observations and experiences. For example, are the quality and quantity of applicants responding to job announcements improving or getting worse? The second way is by monitoring labor-market statistics generated by others.

The most comprehensive source of free data on conditions in the U.S. labor market is the U.S. Bureau of Labor Statistics (BLS). The BLS web site (www.BLS.gov) contains information on wages, productivity, benefits, employment, and unemployment. The BLS also conducts a National Compensation Survey that provides wage and benefit data for more than 400 occupations in more than 80 metropolitan and non-metropolitan areas in the United States. Recent BLS projections are for an acceptable balance of labor supply and demand on a nationwide, all-industry basis, but shortages and surpluses are projected in some occupations and industries. This means that some firms will need to extend workforce plans three to five years out to accommodate training time and alternative sourcing for hard-to-fill positions, while other firms with sufficient talent pipelines can focus on more short-term planning.[21]

Many sources of labor-market information and forecasts exist. Table 5 summarizes some of the most popular sources and their web addresses.

Table 5. Sources of Labor-Market Forecasts and Related Information

- Conference Board Help Wanted Advertising Index: www.conference-board.org
- Empire State Manufacturing Survey: www.ny.frb.org
- ISM Report on Business: www.ism.ws
- Labor Market Information by State: www.bls.gov/bls/ofolist.htm
- Manpower Employment Outlook Survey: www.manpower.com/press/meos.cfm
- Monster Employment Index: www.monsterworldwide.com
- NFIB Small Business Poll: www.nfib.com
- SHRM Leading Indicators of National Employment Index: www.shrm.org/line
- TrimTabs Online Jobs Postings Index: www.trimtabs.com
- U.S. Bureau of Labor Statistics: www.BLS.gov
- U.S. Census Bureau: www.census.gov
- Local Employment Dynamics from the U.S. Census Bureau: lehd.did.census.gov/led

---

It can also be helpful to identify and track trends that might affect future labor-supply quality or quantity. Companies such as Microsoft watch college-enrollment trends and have expressed concern about the number of U.S. students pursuing computer science degrees. Kevin Schofield, general manager of strategy and communications at Microsoft Research, states, "We want to make sure that there's a rich pipeline of great talent that we can hire to build fantastic products, in our own company and in our partners' companies as well, because it's about the whole industry and not just the products that Microsoft owns itself."[22]

Financial-services company Capital One develops three-year labor-demand forecasts by anticipating business drivers and changes that will impact its headcount needs. Proprietary forecast models determine what its maximum sustainable size is in any given market. By analyzing factors such as the population in the area that might apply to Capital One and demographic trends, it estimates what percentage of the population is likely to apply to Capital One over time. It then determines what percentage of applicants are likely to receive job offers and calculates when its labor reservoir will be depleted to the point that it can't hire enough people, which becomes its long-term maximum sustainable size around which it plans its expansion strategy. Capital One also does a zip-code analysis of employees in the area to determine be optimum areas in which to locate, so that it doesn't lose existing employees to new sites.[23] Some health care companies have even developed their own nursing schools and partner with other educational programs such as radiology schools. This helps to ensure a flow of applicants by allowing the students to work as interns/externs and to become aligned with the organization.

Resolving Gaps Between Labor Supply and Labor Demand

The next step in the workforce planning process is to compare the forecasted demand for labor in terms of quality, quantity, and skills mix with the anticipated numbers and skills of the organization's current workforce to identify talent surpluses or shortages and to estimate future hiring needs. Comparing labor-supply and labor-demand forecasts may indicate a projected equilibrium, in which the organization expects to have the amount and quality of labor necessary to meet its future staffing needs. Alternatively, a projected surplus of labor, in which case the organization expects to have more employees than it will need, or a projected labor shortage, in which case it will need to reassign workers internally or hire new employees from outside the organization, are also possible. If either a labor surplus or labor shortage is forecast, an action plan should be developed to proactively address the anticipated surplus or shortage of employees so that jobs are always filled by the right number of the right kinds of employees. Action plans should always be consistent with the firm's business strategy, talent philosophy, and HR strategy. For example, layoffs are inconsistent with a talent philosophy of wanting people to contribute to the company over long-term careers and an HR strategy of developing and retaining talent able to contribute to the firm over time, and they often result in negative outcomes for the firm. Increasing overtime or part-time work, hiring freezes, transferring work to less busy units, increasing workers' productivity, and increasing the use of temporary or contract workers can all be a part of an action plan.

A steering committee developed an action plan to address the nurse shortage in the United States. Here is a portion of the action plan they developed:[24]

- *Communicate nursing's economic value*—educate the public about nursing's pivotal role in health care.

- *Improve the work environment*—so that quality patient care is optimized and professional nursing staff is retained.
- *Communicate the professional nursing culture*—asserting nursing's high standards of professional practice, education, leadership, and collaboration to better appeal to potential nurses and enhance nursing's image and nurses' career satisfaction.
- *Education*—reshape nursing education to enhance nursing's image.
- *Recruitment/retention*—enhance professional opportunities to attract and sustain excellent nurses for long, rewarding careers.

Stu Reed, senior vice president, Integrated Supply Chain, Motorola Inc., developed an action plan to increase the future supply of supply chain managers. Motorola first identified the likely career path and skills the supply chain professional of the future needs to get to the top job. The company then partnered aggressively with key supply chain schools in North America and internationally. "We validate our model with them and let them know what type of graduates we need for them to provide us," said Reed.[25] By working backward through their supply chain for talent, Motorola has increased the future supply of supply chain managers with the skills it will need to be successful.

Whenever changes are observed in labor-market conditions, it is important to try to assess whether the change represents a labor-market trend that is likely to continue or whether it is a shorter-term fluctuation caused by the business cycle. Understanding whether a shortage or surplus of applicants is the result of temporary factors or whether it reflects a trend that is likely to continue is important because different staffing strategies are appropriate for each.[26] Action plans may need to address labor surpluses or shortages that are temporary or persistent in nature. We will discuss each next.

Temporary Talent Shortage

What should be done if a shortage of qualified talent is thought to be temporary? Offering hiring incentives (such as sign-on bonuses) and retention bonuses (such as stock options), or cash to be paid after the employee has successfully worked with the company for a certain period of time, can help to hire and retain qualified employees. Because higher salaries cost the organization more money for the duration of the new hire's tenure with the company, it is often better to offer hiring inducements that last only as long as the talent shortage. This limits the increased costs to only when they are needed to attract scarce talent.[27] When companies find it difficult to hire in a tight labor market, they often turn to more expensive recruiting methods such as additional advertising and search firms, or they lower their hiring standards so that more recruits are considered qualified for the position. Neither of these strategies is guaranteed to work, and each might produce unwanted consequences. More expensive recruiting methods may quickly drain a recruiting budget without resulting in an acceptable hire, and lowering hiring standards decreases the quality and stability of the company's workforce, which may not be acceptable.

If a shortage of employees is expected, people currently working for the company may be able to fill some of the positions, but others will likely still have to be filled by new hires. Because forecasted shortages have implications for planning for the training and development of employees, workforce planning should be integrated with planning for employee development. If the root cause of a projected labor shortage is unusually high turnover, the action plan should address the cause of the turnover (e.g., low pay, poor supervision, limited career-advancement potential, limited training opportunities, etc.). Employee surveys and informal discussions with managers and key employees can help to uncover the reasons for high turnover and allow the company to address its causes. In some cases, creativity may be needed to resolve projected labor shortages. For example, when H&R Block had trouble finding workers for its technical support call center in suburban Kansas City, it relocated the facility to the inner city and hired workers who lived downtown.[28]

Persistent Talent Shortage

If it is likely that a worker shortage will last a number of years, an organization must reduce its demand for the talents that will be in short supply and/or increase the supply of the qualifications it needs. Although it can be possible to increase the supply of needed talent, this is not a fast or practical solution for most organizations. Instead, many organizations try to reduce their need for skills that will be in short supply by increasing their use of automation and technology, and by redesigning jobs so that fewer people with the desired talent are needed.

The petroleum industry is facing a severe shortage of petroleum engineers, geologists, and geophysicists, despite automating some processes and reducing the number of workers needed in some jobs from three to one. Despite the decrease in needed workers due to greater automation, the personnel shortage is so serious that Peter Schwartz, former head of business environment at Royal Dutch/Shell, states that it "will ultimately slow the rate of innovation as we need it more and more. Eventually, it means we'll get less oil."[29]

Canadian power generation and wholesale company TransAlta provides a good example of strategic staffing planning in this type of environment.[30] To forecast and plan for the next five to 10 years, TransAlta began by reviewing past attrition rates and hiring profiles for its western Canadian workforce during the previous seven years. Local leaders also provided input into the forecasts and plans. By comparing those findings with TransAlta's growth plans and the evolving labor market, TransAlta gauged the balance it will have to strike between recruiting new employees and enhancing the skills of its existing staff. A key challenge TransAlta identified is that the Canadian workforce is growing at only half the rate of the overall population; within the next decade or so, the workforce will actually decline because of retiring Baby Boomers. It also expects competition for skilled workers to intensify further because of increased demand from nearby competitors for the same skills. TransAlta's leaders recognized that failing to address these challenges would mean a productivity drop, and they did not want that to happen.

For each of its facilities, TransAlta created action plans for attracting and recruiting new employees, retaining existing employees, maintaining or, preferably, improving productivity, and capturing and transferring key areas of knowledge before people retire. The high cost of living in Fort McMurray, and the competitiveness of compensation packages offered by the petroleum industry, presented special challenges. Because losing experienced employees compromises TransAlta's ability to operate efficiently, retention is an important goal. To enhance the retention of seasoned employees in this location it is considering strategic measures ranging from additional mortgage assistance to help offset the high cost of local housing to hiring workers earlier than needed to ensure the complete transfer of knowledge from experienced staff. To ensure that it keeps on top of local changes, TransAlta also updates all data every two years as part of its regular assets review.[31]

If talent is hard to find or is too expensive, one option is to out-source the affected business process. Business-process outsourcing is the relocation of an entire business function, including production, manufacturing, or customer service, to an independent service provider, which may be in the same or a different country. Commonly outsourced business functions include IT and technology services, customer service, and even corporate training. If the firm is able to maintain or improve the quality of the business process being outsourced, outsourcing can enable a firm to focus on its core competencies and strategic issues, and to reduce costs.

The relationship between $3.7 billion transportation-services com-pany Penske Corporation and the business-process outsourcing firm Genpact involves more than 30 different business processes and illus-trates how some companies are engaging in business-process outsourc-ing and leveraging offshore skilled labor. To reduce costs and improve the quality of its operations, independent Genpact essentially acts as Penske's virtual subsidiary. When a Penske truck is leased for an inter-state trip, Genpact's staff in India check the customer's credit and ac-quire permits. If the truck is stopped at a weigh station because it lacks a required fuel permit, Indian workers transmit the necessary document to the weigh station to get the vehicle back on the road within a half hour. After a trip, the driver's log is shipped to a Genpact facility in Juarez, Mexico, where mileage, tax, toll, and fuel data are entered into Penske computers and processed in India. When Penske sells the truck, staff in Mexico record the transaction.[32]

When a firm cannot find the quantity and/or quality of talent that it needs, it may have the option of automating the job and reducing its need for employees with the scarce talent. Companies including Home Depot, Costco, Wal-Mart, and many supermarkets have installed self-service checkout lanes, and many callers to customer-service departments now receive automated responses to their inquiries. Not all jobs can be automated, but it is frequently an option for companies facing talent shortages or wanting to reduce their labor costs by getting the same work done with fewer employees. Automation may generate the need for new and specific types of skills, and this must be considered to ensure the automation functions properly.

Temporary Employee Surplus

When a firm expects a business slowdown to be temporary, it has several options. If slowdowns are cyclical or happen frequently, using temporary or contingent workers, who are the first to be let go when business slows, can help to provide a buffer around key permanent workers and provide them greater employment security. Temporary layoffs are another option to deal with a short-term employee surplus, but they may need to last more than six months to be cost-effective due to severance costs,[33] greater unemployment insurance premiums, temporary productivity declines, and the rehiring and retraining process. Losing the investments the organization has already made in hiring and training the laid-off workers can also be costly. Alternatives to layoffs include across-the-board salary cuts or a reduction in work hours, or reallocating workers to expanding areas of the business. Some firms offer unpaid vacations, sabbaticals, job sharing, and other creative solutions to temporary surpluses.

Persistent Employee Surplus

Organizations sometimes need to permanently reduce the number of people they employ. Technology changes, the entrance of competitors, and changes in customer preferences can fundamentally change the number and types of workers an organization needs. Early retirement incentives, layoffs, and not filling vacated positions can all reduce an employer's headcount, but not without a cost. Early retirement programs can result in the most skilled and productive employees leaving the organization. In addition, they can result in significant increases in retirement plan costs and funding. Not filling vacated positions can leave key positions in the organization unstaffed or understaffed. Layoffs can damage workforce morale and hurt the firm's reputation as an employer. Action plans to address a persistent employee surplus may also involve reassignments, hiring freezes, and steering employees away from careers in that position to reduce the need for future layoffs. Retraining employees to fill other jobs in the firm can help bring labor supply and demand into balance.

The goal of any staffing strategy is to acquire and retain the most productive employees and eliminate lower performers. Planning activities that enable an organization to anticipate its future employment needs and scale down gradually through mass layoffs or dramatic restructuring can help to control restructuring costs and retain top performers.

Staffing Planning

In addition to workforce planning, it is also important to take the time to plan the staffing process itself. The three questions that need to be answered are:

1. How many people should be recruited?
2. What resources are needed?
3. How much time will it take to hire?

We address each of these questions next.

How Many People Should Be Recruited?

Because some job candidates will usually lose interest in the position before being hired and others will lack appropriate qualifications, it is almost always necessary to generate more applicants than the number of open positions. Additionally, having greater numbers of applicants allows an organization to be more selective, allowing it to identify the candidate who best fits the position (rather than hiring the only person who applies). At the same time, recruiting solely to reach numerical applicant targets misses the resource preservation goal of recruiting only the number of applicants necessary to meet hiring goals.

The "ideal" number of applicants to recruit for an opening depends on the nature of the organization's staffing and HR strategies. Although a recruiting pool that is too small risks being unable to identify enough qualified candidates to be able to fill all of the openings, a pool that is too large places unreasonable burdens on the recruiting function's administrative systems and wastes time and money. Additionally, generating a large pool of applicants does not guarantee that recruits will have the appropriate qualifications, and risks ill will among the many rejected applicants.

Attending to applicant quality is also critical: If the bottom half of the talent that exists for a job is all that applies to an organization, below-average talent is all the organization will be able to hire. The goal is to attract a sufficient number of candidates who meet or exceed the personal and technical requirements of the job to be able to fill all of the job openings.

Staffing Yields. The best source of information for determining how many people to recruit comes from data collected during a company's previous recruiting efforts. One way to start is by understanding previous staffing yields, or the proportion of applicants moving from one stage of the hiring process to the next, and hiring yields (also called selection ratios), or the percent of applicants ultimately hired. For example, as illustrated in Figure 6, if three out of four job offers are typically accepted, 100 offers will be required to yield 75 hires. If, on average, one job offer is made for every four interviews, then 400 candidates must be interviewed to generate 100 job offers. If four out of five invitations to interview are accepted, then 500 invitations must be issued to produce the 400 interview candidates. If one out of every four applicants is typically invited for an interview, then 2,000 applicants must be generated, resulting in a selection ratio of 3.125 percent (75 hires out of 2,000 applicants). Staffing-yield pyramids like the one in Figure 6 can be constructed to illustrate these requirements based on the organization's previous experience, and spreadsheets greatly simplify their calculation and application.

Figure 6. Staffing-Yields Pyramid

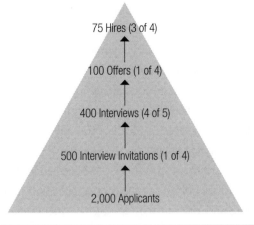

75 Hires (3 of 4)

100 Offers (1 of 4)

400 Interviews (4 of 5)

500 Interview Invitations (1 of 4)

2,000 Applicants

Staffing-yield estimates are only relevant for the same type of hires and assume comparable labor-market conditions. These ratios are not consistent across all jobs, hiring situations, or economic conditions. For example, Microsoft only hires about two percent of its applicants for software positions, which is typical for its industry.[34] On the other hand, organizations such as Amway and Discovery Toys hire the majority of their applicants for sales-representative positions. Offer acceptance rates are also generally lower for professional and technical candidates than for unskilled and semiskilled workers in a favorable local labor market. Staffing yields can vary widely across industries, and even within an industry. A company's yields tend to be reasonably consistent from year to year, however, and sometimes trends can be identified that add to the accuracy of prediction when other market conditions are taken into account.[35] For example, if an organization has made its salary levels more competitive or even higher than the market, it can generally expect a larger applicant pool and a lower percentage of applicants hired as a result. At the very least, prior staffing yields can be a good starting point for estimating probable yields and minimum applicant quantity requirements for the current recruiting effort.

A primary disadvantage of relying on past staffing yields to forecast recruiting needs is that, ideally, an organization will be able to improve on past yield ratios by analyzing the effectiveness of different recruiting sources, targeting recruiting efforts at the most productive sources, and identifying and leveraging the recruiting methods that work best for the given job and organization. However, if the applicant pool an organization attracts is of higher quality than it has been in the past, then it can recruit fewer applicants yet enjoy even greater hiring success with greater yield and selection ratios. This will allow it to hire a greater percentage of applicants who become successful in their jobs and raise the average performance level of the workforce.

It is important to remember that the key issue is not whether staffing yields are high or low. What matters is whether the staffing system is producing the right numbers of the right kinds of employees in the right time frame. Although staffing is an investment, not an expense, a key issue for many organizations is the need to control its monetary investment in staffing. This can be accomplished by limiting the size of the applicant pool or by more efficiently managing the application process. If the proportion of high-potential applicants increases, the total number of applicants needed to generate the right number of the right quality new hires decreases, reducing the cost of applicant processing and assessment. In contrast, in the past, a key assumption of applicant-selection techniques has been that larger applicant pools are superior to smaller pools, because recruiting larger numbers of applicants increases the odds that high-potential recruits would be in the applicant pool. This assumption does not necessarily hold true. Smaller applicant pools may be superior when recruiting yields and costs are considered.

For example, assume that an organization wants to hire the best talent it can find (say, the top 10 percent of the talent in a given field) and that the organization's applicant-assessment methods are able to flawlessly assess the talent of each applicant (not likely, but let's assume). In this case, an organization would traditionally try to generate as many applicants as it could and hire one-tenth of them, producing a low hiring ratio (probably 10 percent, assuming an even sampling of the total talent). Accordingly, it has traditionally been thought that a low hiring ratio (i.e., hiring only 10 percent of applicants) was required to secure the best talent because the large applicant pool is assumed to increase the chances that the top talent is in the applicant pool to be identified by the selection system. In fact, the lower the hiring ratio, the higher the presumed quality of talent. This can be true, but it assumes that the applicants are truly reflective of the entire spectrum of talent. To the extent that a disproportionate number of undesirable applicants apply, the key assumption of this recruiting strategy is invalid and an even lower hiring ratio is required to add talent in the top 10 percent to the organization (if they have added to the organization at all).

A better strategy would be to increase the number of high-potential applicants and decrease the number of low-potential applicants. If an organization is able to do this effectively, it will be able to increase the quality of its hires while simultaneously increasing its staffing yields and getting a better return on its recruiting investment. Thus, a lower hiring ratio does not always reflect higher quality talent once the recruiting system is taken into consideration.

Organizations sometimes seek to obtain high yields (hiring a large percentage of applicants) in the recruiting function to keep costs down, but this often occurs without considering the potential dilution of an organization's talent. If applicant quality is not simultaneously considered, high hiring yields can be detrimental to effective recruitment and selection. However, if an organization leverages the recruitment methods and sources that work best for it, it may be able to alter the talent distribution of its applicant pool to contain only the best of the available talent (e.g., the upper 50 percent in quality). In this case, a much higher targeted recruiting yield (say 30 percent) could produce the same quality of new hires as did a lower 10-percent yield under the traditional method when a greater number of undesirable candidates were included in the applicant pool. Hiring the best five of 50 applicants who are poor fits with the job and organization is less ideal than hiring the best five of 20 applicants who are good fits with the job and organization.

For many organizations, one of the goals of a strategic-staffing effort should be to increase staffing yields (i.e., fewer applicants are weeded out during the hiring process resulting in hiring a greater percentage of applicants thus reducing costs) while also increasing the qualifications and talents of the resulting hires. This approach puts great demands on the organization's ability to maintain a high-quality applicant pool. One advantage of investing in increasing the quality of the applicant pool is that if the quality of the applicant pool increases, the demands placed on the applicant-assessment and selection systems decrease as more of the applicants are likely to be successful hires. Additionally, it is important to remember that even the best applicant-assessment system cannot identify potential high performers if they never apply to the organization. Targeted recruiting efforts increase the probability that the top candidates apply, which is a critical step in their ultimately becoming employees. The time and financial resources invested in recruiting and evaluating each candidate is also less likely to be wasted if better recruiting results in a greater proportion of initial applicants being good fits with the position and the organization, and who are likely to accept job offers should they be extended.

Staffing yields from different recruiting sources should be evaluated for staffing planning purposes. The quantity and quality of hires from various recruiting sources are likely to differ both within and across organizations. One company may be able to hire good performers from newspaper advertisements, while this strategy may be ineffective for another company or for the same company in a different geographic location. Determining which recruiting sources are the "best" to use generally varies also with the nature of the position and its level within the organization. The Internet may be a very effective recruiting source for information technology hires, but less effective for clerical support or manufacturing jobs. Recruiters are likely to differ in their annual hiring rates and the quality of their hires. If an organization needs to hire quickly, it is very helpful for it to know how long it has typically taken to fill positions from a variety of sources so that it can strategically choose among them.

If an organization did not collect the relevant information during previous staffing efforts, the estimation of staffing yields becomes more challenging, but is not impossible. Benchmarking competing organizations may be insightful, and some of the sources of recruits (e.g., headhunting agencies, college placement offices) may be able to provide some information on the average yield ratios of their candidates. This information is not ideal, however, as it is not specific to the company and job in question. Characteristics of the company itself, including its competitive position, location, compensation package, image, and local quality of life and recreation opportunities are likely to dramatically influence staffing yields.

What Resources Are Needed?

In addition to identifying the desired number of applicants and appropriate goals for each stage of the recruiting process, it is also important to identify the resources and size of the recruiting staff that will be necessary to secure the desired number of hires. We next discuss two methods of estimating needed resources for a staffing effort: workload-driven forecasting and staffing efficiency-driven forecasting.

Workload-Driven Forecasting. Workload-driven forecasting uses historical data on the average number of hires typically made per recruiter or the average number of recruits processed per recruiter over a given period (e.g., week, month, or year) to forecast the number of recruiters that will be needed for the current effort. For example, referring again to Figure 6, if an organization's average recruiter can process 100 recruits during a recruiting drive, it will need a staff of 20 recruiters to manage the targeted 2,000 recruits. Similar procedures can be used to estimate the amount of additional resources (e.g., telephone costs, advertising costs, photocopying, background checks, medical tests, etc.) that will be needed for the staffing effort. This approach focuses on managing recruiter workloads based on the organization's historical recruiting performance, and can be a good place to begin estimating the resources needed for the current effort. The amount of money that needs to be budgeted for the staffing effort also depends on factors including the number of people to be hired, whether recruits are local or from far away, the recruiting sources used, the selection methods employed, and the tightness of the labor market.

Staffing Efficiency-Driven Forecasting. Another method of forecasting how many recruiters are needed is based on staffing efficiency. Staffing efficiency[36] is the total cost (both internal, such as recruiters, and external, such as job posting fees) associated with the amount of new-hire compensation (the total starting base pay of all new starting employees). For example, if internal- and external-staffing costs were $100,000 for the recruitment of $600,000 of total compensation (e.g., 10 people with starting base salaries of $60,000), then the staffing efficiency would be 100,000/600,000, or 16.67 percent. Lower staffing-efficiency percentages indicate that costs are a lower proportion of total base compensation recruited, and reflect greater staffing efficiency. An organization can use staffing efficiency in forecasting the necessary staffing budget and number of recruiters it will need by setting a maximum staffing-efficiency ratio for its upcoming hiring effort. For example, if the organization is targeting 25 new hires per month at an average starting base salary of $50,000 and a staffing-efficiency ratio of 15 percent or less, it will have a budget of $187,500 (25 x $50,000 x 0.15) a month to spend on recruiters and other staffing resources.[37] The staffing-efficiency approach to forecasting recruiting staff and resources is financially- and efficiency-driven rather than workload-driven, and can be a useful metric for evaluating changes in staffing efficiency over time.

Staffing Cost Estimates. The Saratoga Institute[38] includes six basic elements to calculate the cost of external hiring:

1. Advertising expenses;
2. Agency and search firm fees;
3. Employee referral bonuses;

4. Recruiter and applicant travel costs;
5. Relocation costs; and
6. Company recruiter costs (prorated salary and benefits if the recruiter performs duties other than staffing).

These six factors account for 90 percent of the costs to hire. Saratoga Institute adds an additional 10 percent to cover miscellaneous expenses, including testing, reference checking, hiring-manager time, and administrative support.[39]

The internal cost-per-hire calculation is very similar, and includes four elements:[40]

1. Internal advertising costs;
2. Travel and interview costs;
3. Relocation costs; and
4. Internal recruiter costs.

Combining forecasts of both external- and internal-hiring costs provides an estimate of the total cost of a staffing effort.

How Much Time Will It Take to Hire?

Staffing often takes longer than expected. Hiring managers don't want jobs to be vacant any longer than necessary, but it takes time to find, screen, and negotiate with each new hire. Establishing a staffing timeline before beginning the staffing initiative ensures that hiring managers,

Figure 7. Sample of Cumulative Yield Time Requirements

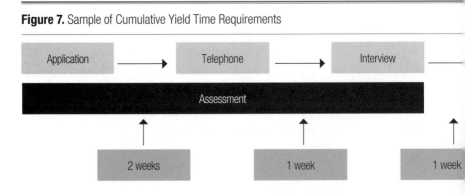

recruiters, and other staffing specialists know what to expect. Time-lapse information on the average interval between application and interview, interview to offer, offer to hire, etc., can be useful for timeline-development purposes, allowing us to identify daily, weekly, and monthly goals for each staffing step. Technology (e.g., resume software and accepting job applications over the Internet) can greatly impact how long each staffing stage lasts, and it is a good idea to regularly update the expected timeline to adjust for unexpected efficiencies and delays.

The length of each staffing stage varies widely across jobs and organizations. In general, higher-level positions take longer to fill than lower-level positions, but skill shortages and local competition can lengthen the time-to-fill for lower-level positions as well. Figure 7 illustrated a typical pattern of cumulative lead-time requirements.

Throughout the staffing process, reliable, accurate progress reports should be prepared and compared to the staffing plan. It could be that some stages of the staffing process take longer or shorter than projected, and the projected timeline should be adjusted accordingly. Maintaining progress reports also helps track whether the current number of hires is on track to produce the total number of hires the organization is striving for within the targeted period of time. If the current hiring pace is found to be too slow to meet the hiring targets, the organization may be able to take steps to speed up the process or recruit more people than it had initially intended.

If it is known that job openings are likely to exist, based on historical turnover or hiring patterns, the recruiting staff can begin sourcing and

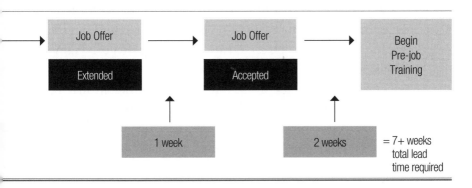

processing candidates before the positions even become available. This can dramatically reduce the time it takes to hire someone to fill an opening because recruits are already in the pipeline. For example, assume that an organization knows that it has seven percent annual turnover in a key sales-representative position in which it staffs 100 employees. If it does not expect any changes in this pattern in the upcoming year, the organization can plan to fill seven sales-representative vacancies in the next 12 months. If the company starts recruiting people for the position now, it is more likely that recruits who are good fits with the job and organization will be located and enticed to apply. By having candidates already engaged in the hiring process, the time-to-fill can be relatively quick.

This approach is called "continuous recruiting" and is particularly useful for positions with relatively high turnover (because openings will need to be filled throughout the year on a rolling basis), for jobs that typically have a long time-to-fill, or for jobs that cost the organization a lot of money while they are vacant (because the time-to-fill will be shortened, thus reducing the cost associated with the position being vacant). With continuous recruiting, cut-scores are often used to make hiring decisions to ensure that minimum qualifications for the position are met. "Batch recruiting," in contrast, involves the development of a new applicant pool every time the organization has one or more positions to fill, typically resulting in a longer time-to-fill.

If organizations in a particular industry tend to recruit on the same cycle, a job-centric staffing philosophy may reduce the quantity of available talent. For example, if engineering companies tend to start their college recruiting in November and confirm new hires in March, waiting until a job opening occurs in March to begin recruiting for a replacement may mean that an organization is forced to recruit from the other organizations' rejected job candidates. Recruiting after competing organizations do may work for an organization using a low-cost strategy that is not looking for top-tier talent, but other organizations may be unable to identify a sufficient number of quality applicants because they are recruiting out-of-cycle with their competitors.

Summary

Forecasting the number, types, and quality of employees needed to execute the business strategy is critical for effective staffing. Setting talent goals and objectives that are consistent with the firm's staffing strategy and talent philosophy are important goals of the planning process. The assessment of the organization's external labor environment and a company's own talent strengths and shortcomings can influence its competitive advantage and the business strategies it is likely to be able to pursue successfully.

It is important to determine the size of the recruiting staff and resources that will be needed, and to secure the appropriate budget and resources before the staffing initiative begins. Additionally, it is important for planning purposes that the timeline for the recruiting effort be established to ensure that the correct number of new hires will be ready to start when they are needed. Although this is obviously particularly critical before an expansion effort or the hiring of an unusually large number of people, it is also important to assess needed resources before hiring a single individual to ensure that hiring goals can be met and that the hiring manager understands what to expect from the staffing process.

Endnotes

[1] See Phillips, J.M. & Gully, S.M. *Strategic Staffing*, 2009. Upper Saddle River, NJ: Prentice Hall.

[2] Handfield-Jones, H., Michaels, E., & Axelrod, B., "Talent Management: A Critical Part of Every Leader's Job," *Ivey Business Journal*, November/December 2001, reprint #9B01TF09, p. 6.

[3] Johnson, W.B., and Packer, A.E., *Workforce 2000: Work and Workers for the 21st Century*, 1987, Indianapolis: Hudson Institute, Inc.

[4] Butler, J.E., Ferris, G.R., & Napier, N.K., *Strategy and Human Resources Management*, 1991, Cincinnati: South-Western.

[5] Prahalad, C.K. & Bettis, R.A., "The Dominant Logic: A New Linkage Between Diversity and Performance." *Strategic Management Journal*, 1986, 7, 485-501.

[6] Butler, Ferris, & Napier, 1991.

[7] Bechet, T.P. & Walker, L.W., "Aligning Staffing With Business Strategy," *Human Resource Planning*, 1993, 16, pp. 1-16.

[8] Ibid.

[9] Agrawal, V., Manyika, J.M., & Richards, J.E., "Matching People to Jobs," *The McKinsey Quarterly*, 2003 Number 2.

[10] Karpinski, R., "Cisco Attempts to Boost B2B Sales," *Internetweek*, March 16, 2001. Available online at: www.internetweek.com/story/INW20010316S0003). Accessed July 9, 2008.

[11] Bond, G., "Jobs Lost as High Dollar Hits Exporters," *The New Zealand Herald*, January 24, 2006. Available online at: www.nzherald.co.nz/section/story.cfm?c_id=1&objectid=10365097. Accessed January 14, 2009.

[12] Schneider, C., "The New Human-Capital Metrics," *CFO Magazine*, February 15 2006. Available online at: www.cfo.com/article.cfm/5491043/1/c_2984284?f=archives. Accessed January 14, 2009.

[13] Heneman, H.G. III. & Sandver, M.H. (1977), "Markov Analysis in Human Resource Administration: Applications and Limitations," *Academy of Management Review*, 2, 535-42.

[14] New York State Department of Civil Service, "Management and Mobility: Part III – Using Existing Tools," *Work Force and Succession Planning*, September 2002. Available online at: www.cs.state.ny.us/successionplanning/workgroups/ ManagementandMobility/skillsinventory.html. Accessed: January 14, 2009.

[15] Malykhina, E., "Supplying Labor to Meet Demand," *InformationWeek*, March 21, 2005. Available online at: www.informationweek.com/story/showArticle. jhtml?articleID=159902302. Accessed January 11, 2009.

[16] Ibid.

[17] Weber, M., "The Labor Pool Becomes a Supply Chain," *Industrial Management*, July 1, 2006. Available online at: cio.ittoolbox.com/news/display. asp?i=146744&p=1. Accessed August 15, 2008.

[18] Werther, W.B., Jr. & Davis, K., *Human Resources and Personnel Management*, 5th ed., 2005, New York: McGraw-Hill.

[19] Munson, H., "Valuing Experience: How to Motivate and Retain Mature Workers," April 2003. Report #1329-03-RR, The Conference Board.

[20] Schildhouse, J., "Working Hard to Avoid the Labor Shortage," *Inside Supply Management*, March 2006, 17(3), p. 22.

[21] Hansen, F., "Feast and Famine in Recruiting of Professionals," *Workforce Management Online*, April 2006. Available online at: www.workforce.com/ archive/feature/24/34/16/index.php. Accessed March 4, 2009.

[22] "Microsoft Listens to College Students, Faculty as Bill Gates Visits Top IT and Engineering Colleges," *Microsoft Press Pass*, October 12, 2005. Available online at: www.microsoft.com/presspass/features/2005/oct05/10-12Campus.mspx. Accessed January 14, 2009.

[23] Arend, M., "Campus Culture," *Site Selection Magazine*, June 28, 2001.

[24] American Nursing Association, *Nursing's Agenda for the Future*, 2002. Available online at: nursingworld.org/naf/. Accessed July 26, 2008.

[25] Schildhouse, J., "Working Hard to Avoid the Labor Shortage," *Inside Supply Management*, March 2006, 17(3), p. 22.

[26] This section is based in part on Director, S.M. & Collison, J., *Staffing Research: Staffing Strategy Over the Business Cycle*. SHRM Research Report 05-0551, 2005 Alexandria, VA: Society for Human Resource Management.

[27] Ibid.

[28] O'Briant, S.M., "Corporate Giving: More Bang for the Buck," Kiplinger, August 13, 2001, Available online at: special.kiplinger.com/hr/stories/corporate_giving_ br_more_bang_for_the_buck.html.

[29] "Talent Shortage Slows Oil Tech," *Red Herring*, May 14, 2006. Available online at: www.redherring.com/Article.aspx?a=16854&hed=Talent+Shortage+Slows+O il+Tech#. Accessed August 18, 2007.

[30] Phillips & Gully, 2009.

[31] Ibid.

[32] Engardio, P., "Penske's Offshore Partner in India," *BusinessWeek Online*, January 30, 2006. Available online at: www.businessweek.com/magazine/content/06_05/b3969414.htm. Accessed January 13, 2009.

[33] See Rigby, D., "Look Before You Layoff," *Harvard Business Review*, 2002, 80(4), pp. 20-1.

[34] Matloff, N., "Debunking the Myth of a Desperate Software Labor Shortage," Testimony to the U.S. House Judiciary Committee Subcommittee on Immigration. Presented April 21, 1998, updated September 27, 1999.

[35] Hawk, R.H., *The Recruitment Function*, 1967, New York: Academy of Management Association.

[36] See Staffing.org for additional information on this metric.

[37] Burkholder, N., "How Many Recruiters Do We Need and What Happened to Alice?" *Staffing.org*, April 23, 2003. Available online at: www.staffing.org/updates/archive423_000.asp. Accessed August 15, 2008.

[38] For more information, see the Saratoga section of the PricewaterhouseCoopers web site at: www.pwc.com/extweb/service.nsf/docid/0516c36c9a61714985256eba00702ed5.

[39] From Davidson, B., "Hiring an Employee: How Much Does It Cost?" *Workforce.com*. Available online at: www.workforce.com/archive/feature/22/25/58/223946.php. Accessed March 4, 2009.

[40] Ibid.

Index

F

forecasts 15, 27
    exchange rate forecasts 11
    forecast models 32
    interest rate forecasts 11
    labor forecasts 13-14
        labor-demand forecasts 13, 35
        labor-supply forecasts 35
forecasted employees 25
forecasting 1, 2, 3, 28
    forecasting and planning, goals 2
    forecasting information 10
    forecasting period 15, 22
    forecasting techniques 28
    labor-supply forecasting 21, 27
    staffing efficiency-driven forecasting 48, 49
    trend forecasting methods 19
    work-load driven forecasting 48
future talent 10
future trends 21

G

General Electric 3
General Motors 12
Genpact 39
global-talent arena 1
growth strategy 13

H

H&R Block 37
headcount 19
hiring 47
    decisions 52
    effort 49
    freezes 35, 41
    goals 6, 53
    incentives 36
    needs 35
    patterns 51
    process 44, 52
    rates 48
    ratio 46
    standards 37
    yields 44, 47
historical
    data 48
    information 15
    patterns 14, 28
    trends 15, 17, 19
Home Depot 39
housing purchases 13
HR strategy/strategies 8, 35, 43
HR-information systems 29

I

IBM 29
India 39
international recruiting efforts 18
investment 1

J

job announcements 31
job performance 27
job security 12
judgmental forecasting 14, 18, 19

L

labor 8, 9
    costs 15, 40
    demand 3, 5, 11, 12, 14, 15, 16, 17
    forces 27
    market(s) 6, 10, 21, 22, 27, 31, 45, 49
        labor-market conditions 36, 45
        labor-market statistics 31
        labor-market trend 36
        tight labor market 37
    pool 21
    reservoir 33
    shortage(s) 35, 37
    skilled labor 2, 39
    supply 3, 5, 28, 29
layoffs 35, 40, 41
Links, Jack 11

M

managerial judgment 22
Mexico 39
Microsoft 32, 45
Motorola Inc. 36
multiple predictors 15

N

National Compensation Survey 31
New Zealand 11
new-hire compensation 49

O

organizational changes 10
output 14
outsourcing 39
overtime 15, 35

TransAlta 38, 39
transfers 22
transition analysis (Markov analysis) 22, 23, 26, 27
transition matrix 23
transition probability/probabilities 24, 25, 26, 27
    transition probability estimate 27
    transition probability matrix 24, 25, 26
trend analysis 14, 17, 18
turnover 37, 52
    historical 51
    rates 22, 30
    statistics 15
    turnover-trend analysis 17

U

U.S. Bureau of Labor Statistics (BLS) 31
unemployment rate 13, 28
United Parcel Service 10

V

Valero Energy Corporation 17

W

Wal-Mart 39
Whirlpool 13
workforce 38
    analysis 5
    morale 41
    planning 5, 7, 8, 22, 37, 43
        planning process 6-7, 9, 35
    plans 32

Y

yield ratios 48

Z

zip-code analysis 33

Acknowledgments

Wge would like to thank our sons, Ryan and Tyler, for their support and patience while we wrote this book. We would also like to thank Pearson for allowing us to adapt some of the material from our book, *Strategic Staffing*, for use in this series. We also thank the reviewers—especially Laura Ostroff, director of Total Rewards and HRIS, Bon Secours Health System, Inc.—and the SHRM staff for this opportunity and for their suggestions and insights. If you have feedback about this book or if you would like to contact us for any reason, please e-mail us at phillipsgully@gmail.com.

About the Authors

Jean M. Phillips, Ph.D., is an associate professor of human resource management at the School of Management and Labor Relations, Rutgers University. Dr. Phillips is a current or former member of several editorial boards including *Personnel Psychology*, *Journal of Applied Psychology*, and *Journal of Management*. She received the 2004 Cummings Scholar Award from the Organizational Behavior Division of the Academy of Management and was among the top five percent of published authors in two of the top human resource management journals during the 1990s. She is also the co-author of the college textbooks *Managing Now!* (2007) and *Strategic Staffing* (2008) and consults in the areas of recruiting and staffing, linking employee surveys to organizational outcomes, and team effectiveness. She can be reached at phillipsgully@gmail.com

Stanley M. Gully, Ph.D., is an associate professor of human resource management at the School of Management and Labor Relations, Rutgers University. He is a current or former member of the editorial boards of *Academy of Management Journal*, *Journal of Applied Psychology*, *Journal of Organizational Behavior*, and *Journal of Management*. He received multiple awards for his teaching, research, and service, including a research award from the American Society for Training & Development. His paper on general self-efficacy is in the top 10 most read papers in *Organizational Research Methods* and his meta-analysis on cohesion is in the top 3 most cited papers in Small Group Research. He is the co-author of *Strategic Staffing* (2008) and consults in the areas of recruiting and staffing, employee engagement, team effectiveness, and organizational learning interventions. He can be reached at phillipsgully@gmail.com

Additional SHRM-Published Books

The Cultural Fit Factor: Creating an Employment Brand that Attracts, Retains, and Repels the Right Employees
By Lizz Pellet

The Employer's Immigration Compliance Desk Reference
By Gregory H. Siskind

Employment Termination Source Book
By Wendy Bliss and Gene Thornton

The Essential Guide to Workplace Investigations: How to Handle Employee Complaints & Problems
By Lisa Guerin

Hiring Source Book
By Catherine D. Fyock

Hiring Success: The Art and Science of Staffing Assessment and Employee Selection
By Steven Hunt

Human Resource Essentials: Your Guide to Starting and Running the HR Function
By Lin Grensing-Pophal

Leading With Your Heart: Diversity and Ganas for Inspired Inclusion
By Cari M. Dominguez and Jude A. Sotherlund

Outsourcing Human Resources Functions: How, Why, When, and When Not to Contract for HR Services, 2d ed.
By Mary F. Cook and Scott B. Gildner

Smart Policies for Workplace Technologies: Email, Blogs, Cell Phones and More
By Lisa Guerin

Stop Bullying at Work: Strategies and Tools for HR and Legal Professionals
By Teresa A. Daniel

Strategic Staffing: A Comprehensive System for Effective Workforce Planning, 2nd ed.
By Thomas P. Bechet

For these and other SHRM-published books, please visit
www.shrm.org/publications/books/pages/default.aspx.